The Wonderful You

Naimah & Dr. Q
Illustrations by Stephen Adams

AuthorHouse™ LLC
1663 Liberty Drive
Bloomington, IN 47403
www.authorhouse.com
Phone: 1-800-839-8640

© 2014 Naimah & Dr. Q. All rights reserved.

No part of this book may be reproduced, stored in a retrieval system,
or transmitted by any means without the written permission of the author.

Published by AuthorHouse 07/11/2014

ISBN: 978-1-4969-2014-0 (sc)
ISBN: 978-1-4969-2015-7 (e)

Library of Congress Control Number: 2014911055

Any people depicted in stock imagery provided by Thinkstock are models,
and such images are being used for illustrative purposes only.
Certain stock imagery © Thinkstock.

Because of the dynamic nature of the Internet, any web addresses or links contained in this book may have changed since publication and may no longer be valid. The views expressed in this work are solely those of the author and do not necessarily reflect the views of the publisher, and the publisher hereby disclaims any responsibility for them.

A special thanks to my brothers Stephen J. Edwards,
Daryl C. Edwards and our dear friend Iris B. Gordy.
Also a special thanks to our daughters
Kaamilya, Rashaan and Ajeenah.

Pooky Poo cried
under the umbrella tree.
She should have been as happy
as can be.
But somewhere between here
and now,
she had totally forgotten how.

She searched and searched
all through the day.
The spirit of happiness faded away.

She looked for it here.
She looked for it there.
All she could find was more despair.

An elderly beetlebopper cracked,
"Diddly dee, diddly doo,
think of yourself
as the wonderful you.
Hug yourself and say,
'Wonderful, wonderful, wonderful me.'
Act as though you are,
and you will be."

Pooky Poo felt sheer joy
from the start.
Wonderful feelings
flowed through her heart.

She felt much better
than she did before,
but something was missing
that she couldn't ignore.
Pooky Poo confessed
to her reflection
in the lake,
"I'm still afraid,
for goodness' sake."

"Listen to me,"
spouted a giggly frollywok.
"It's not easy sometimes
for you to see.
You can be anything
you dream to be."

"I can be anything?
Really? Anything?
What must I do?"
pleaded Pooky Poo.

The giggly frollywok declared,
"Climb the mountain of courage.
Believe in yourself.
It's all up to you."

Pooky Poo closed her eyes,
imagining that she could
reach the top of the mountain.
A glowing fairy appeared
and guided her up
the dark, twisting trail.

"It worked! I made it
to the top!" she yelled.
A gazillion stars winked
in the night sky
as Pooky Poo wiped
the last tear from her eye.

As she felt better from head to toe, her faith in herself continued to grow.

"Whoopee! Whoopee!" she shouted with glee. "I can be anything that I dream to be."

Pooky Poo heard strange sounds. A pimpersnickle was spinning around and around.

The spinning pimpersnickle whispered
at the end of his spins,
"Loving yourself is
where happiness begins."

So when Pooky Poo played
under the umbrella tree,
she was as happy
as can be.
Somewhere between here
and now,
she finally remembered how.

She remembered
what the age-old beetlebopper
said to do:
"Think of yourself
as the wonderful you."

She remembered
the giggly frollywok's words with glee:
"I can be anything
that I dream to be."

She remembered the message
of the pimpersnickle
at the end his spins:
"Loving yourself
is where happiness begins."

From that day forward, whenever Pooky Poo played under the umbrella tree, she was as *happy* as can be.

My name is _____.

I want to be a _____ when I grow up.

This is my dream:

_____
_____
_____
_____
_____
_____
_____

Made in the USA
Middletown, DE
14 December 2023

45681245R00015